THE FENS AS I SAW THEM
Elijah Wells

The illustrated memoirs of a local fenman

Mildenhall Museum Publications
6 King Street, Mildenhall, Bury St. Edmunds,
Suffolk IP28 7EX

The Trustees of the Mildenhall and District Museum are grateful to Mr. Elijah Wells for allowing publication, for the first time, of these unique memoirs. They are grateful also for the help that has been given by many local individuals and firms in preparing for publication this the first of a series of booklets illustrating the local history of the Mildenhall area.

First published 1976
Reprinted 1983

ISBN: 0 905457 00 5

CONTENTS

PREFACE.

What is written here refers chiefly to an area of the fens about fifteen miles long, three miles each side of the River Lark between Mildenhall and Prickwillow. It is based mainly on facts which I know from personal experience or have heard from my father.

The young people of this age, the year 1957, may perhaps think it strange that I am able to write with such confidence about things that happened nearly one hundred years ago. It will probably be better understood when I say that I am sixty years old and the youngest of a family of nine. My father was forty two years old when I was born. How much I enjoyed hearing the tales he used to tell about things which happened when he was young and things which he had heard from my grandfather of even earlier times. I am confident that he was not a man who would give a false impression if he could help it nor would he pass on a story he did not believe to be true without telling me of its falsehood.

In my early years we lived in the Fens a good half mile from the nearest road and, to reach our home, we had to cross a river by boat or by walking round the sluice gates on a narrow plank, following a footpath, crossing the river again by a narrow bridge and more planks. Even this route in flood time was quite impassable. In the other direction the hard road was more than a mile away and, to reach a village, we had to walk one and half miles on very bad roads, so my father spent most of the winter evenings at home. It was during these long winter evenings, seated by the fireside, that he would tell us stories of what things were like when he was young. You will understand that the face of the earth in this part of the country has changed very much since then; so has the way of living, the kind of work, the hours of work and the whole social system. I am very much of the opinion that if my grandfather could possibly come back and stand in the place where his house was situated he would not know where he was. If he could see men and women dressed as we are today, with our faces shaved clean and using the machines we do now, and in fact the general appearance of mankind, I think it would make him wonder if he had arrived in another world.

Well, I suppose if we were transferred to the middle of the nineteenth century, our impressions would be the same. We should have a slight advantage over him because we are alive and able to read what has been written about the condition of things one hundred years ago and we can talk to old people, some of whom can give good eye witness accounts of things that happened sixty and perhaps seventy years ago. I mention this because what is written hereafter may appear almost unbelievable and very strange to the younger generation of today.

Chapter 1.

HOW WE CAME.

I have tried to recall some of the things that were impressed on my mind when I was young. I distinctly remember my father saying that his grandfather, old Joe Wells, tracked down into the fens from up country, somewhere in Suffolk he thought, but he could not say for sure the name of the place nor for what reason he came. There have been suggestions by other members of the family that he got into some kind of trouble with his master – probably knocked him over or something like that. Not being able to get employment in that district he had to move on somewhere else. Perhaps however he was just a travelling gypsy and having found a place in the fen that was just above water decided to take possession and settle down. My father never confirmed these suggestions although he was quite confident that Old Joe came from the higher land somewhere in Suffolk and settled down about two miles from a small village in Cambridgeshire on the S.E. side of the fens.

Now, according to my calculations, this was somewhere between 1800 and 1810. What did the fens look like at that time? Perhaps your guess is as good as mine but I do feel, with fifty years experience living in the fens and my ancestors before me for three generations, I ought to be able to form some opinion of what it was like. I would imagine it was a jumbled up mass of peat, reeds, osiers, willow trees, rushes, sedges, ditches and dykes. Some places were covered in water and in others the peat was just solid enough to cultivate. On one of these patches of more solid peat my great grandfather settled and built his home. He had very little money, perhaps none at all, so he had to make do with what material was at hand. If he could have bought material for building he would have had great difficulty in getting it to this place. Here I feel we ought to congratulate Old Joe for his ingenuity and skill for, in this wilderness of mud and water, reeds and willows, he set to work to build a house. For bricks he dug square pieces of earth or soil which in that district would be moor or peat. What these were called then I don't know but later they were called turf. These pieces of turf he used in place of bricks and for a chimney he braided some of the long thin osiers together into a funnel shape. Of course he used reed for thatch and osiers for tying it down. I can imagine it looked quite house-shape if not ship-shape. What he used for windows and doors I am not certain. Maybe he had no windows and for a doorway I should think he just left an open space. For a door I should think he made a willow and reed hurdle which he could fix in the open space. After the first summer he had no fuel troubles because turf when dried makes excellent fuel. It does not make much flame and gives out a fair amount of heat and so it was quite suitable for his kind of house.

As for making a living I don't think this was as difficult as it may appear because the fens, if not inhabited very thickly by men, were very thickly populated with fish, wild fowl and other creatures too, such as frogs, snakes, otters and all kinds of vermin. There were ways and means of catching birds and fish of which I will say more later.

How long Joe lived in this house I do not know but sometime later, for some reason or other, he had to move. He was not allowed to settle on this spot for good so he moved about half a mile to the west. Here he had to build again, this time I think with reeds and plaster. This place became known as "Windy Hall".

Joe must have had a wife because here at this spot, under these conditions and amid such surroundings, in this lonely wilderness of marsh and reeds, they brought up a family of five boys and several girls. One these boys, Thomas, was my grandfather. Apparently this was his home all his life.

At that time there were no bicycles and the only way of getting about was by horseback or walking. Grandfather was not rich enough to own a horse and so he had to walk.

This did not stop him from travelling about a bit for he married a girl from quite a distance away. You must understand they did not travel so much by road in those days nor quite how the crow flies. They travelled as nearly as they could from one point to another. This was the reason for so many old footpaths which are not used today. A great many of them have gone out of existence altogether. Boys brought up up in the fens knew the driest parts and the easiest ditches to jump. They were able to pass from one part of the district to another in the quickest possible time. I can easily imagine my grandfather as a young man tramping on a Sunday across that swampy mass of mud and water, jumping a ditch here, crossing a drain there on a plank or tree trunk, swerving this way and that to avoid a patch of water, and eventually reaching the higher land, passing along footpaths until he came to a road.

Even then it was not easy going because only horsedrawn vehicles travelled along the roads, leaving footmarks,and wheeltracks, which made them very unlevel. Perhaps he thought it worth it if grandmother was waiting for him when he reached his destination. I would rather think he had to have one or two drinks before he tackled the homeward journey.

What a horrible feeling it must have been to leave the girl behind and tramp for miles, especially when it was dark and raining or snowing, across that dreary wilderness. He would not be lonely because he would probably disturb an otter when crossing one of the drains, causing it to whistle and hiss; ducks would flutter and quack as they rose from a patch of water. There would be the continual call of plovers as they circled around after being disturbed from the drier parts of the land.

Well, I don't know how many times grandfather did this before he got his wife; eventually to the best of my knowledge they did settle down to a happy and comfortable life at "Windy Hall". From what my father has told me

I believe the old wind-driven water pumping mills were at this time at the height of their glory, or shall we say in full swing. It was by managing one of these mills that grandfather obtained a basic wage for a livelihood. Maybe you think it was not a very lively place to live but I can assure you they had some very exciting times down there sometimes. The mills had to be kept running when necessary, day and night, Sunday and weekday, if there was enough wind to make them go. Whilst the wind kept in one direction and did not vary in strength there was not much to do so I think this was an easy job, although it was necessary to keep an eye on the weather and watch out for storms or a change in the wind. To occupy his spare time, and to supplement his wages, grandfather would catch birds and fish. To catch birds he made nets and hingles, and sometimes used a gun – the old-fashioned muzzle loading gun. To catch fish he used nets and grigs. Some of the nets for birds and fish he used by day and some by night.

I remember my father telling a story about his catching a pheasant which at that time was worth three shillings alive, two and sixpence dead. He took it home and packed it in a basket for grandmother to take to the village and sell. Off she went with the basket and pheasant and, when she had nearly reached the village, somehow the pheasant got out and flew away. Grandmother was no fool. She watched where it settled and went home and told grandfather who picked up the gun and went off after it. After hunting about, by luck or skill, he managed to put up and shoot it. So away grandmother had to go again with the pheasant, although after all this it had gone down sixpence in value.

By the working of the mills the fens were being drained. Gradually more land was appearing above water and the higher parts were getting more solid. By deepening the drains and cutting more ditches and sock grips the land was getting more workable. It was found that cutting and drying off this peaty soil and selling it for fuel was a good paying business. Also when it was possible to dig deep enough below the peat in some places there was found clay substance which, when mixed with the peaty top-soil, made the land very good for growing wheat and other crops. These changes coming along about the same time began to make the fen a busy place. Not only was work found for men in the villages bordering the fen but farming was made profitable for the owners of the land.

I think my grandmother must have been a very thrifty woman and I believe it was chiefly due to this that they were later able to buy a piece of land and keep two or three cows and a donkey. I never heard of grandfather working for anyone else except for looking after the mill. (By the way at that time it would be called running the mill.) It was amid all this my father was born for Tom and his wife brought up a family of five boys and two girls. My father was the youngest but one. He was called Elijah. The first twenty years of his life he lived at "Windy Hall". Here, with his father and brothers, he learned how to run a mill, to use a spade and scoop, to dig turf and clay, to cut drains and ditches, how to make nets, grigs and hingles and how to use them too. There was not much in the poaching line he could not tell me, from tickling a tench to running down a partridge. Living near the water as he did he learned to skate, and to skate fast, which seemed to be the fashion in those days.

What a happy time they must have had. I think I would have enjoyed it. I feel sure my father did from what he has told me. During this period he fell in love with a girl who lived in one of the nearby villages. At the age of twenty he married and took this beautiful girl (I am sure she must have been beautiful then because she was still beautiful thirty years later and she was my mother) to live in one of the windmills that were made for a house as well as a mill. This was further into the fens and a much more out of the way place than "Windy Hall". The nearest village, a very small one, was about three miles away.

The author and his wife outside their home. The eel traps are now on display in Mildenhall Museum.

Floods at Isleham Sluice March 1937.

A dredger at work in 1916. The author is the second from the left.

The prosperity of the fens grew. The need for draining the land became more apparent and about this time the steam engine was beginning to take the place of the windmill. So my father made a living by running the mill in winter and in his spare time making baskets and eel grigs from the osiers that were plentiful in the fen. He also made the old-fashioned beeskips that were made of straw and osiers. This he did in winter but in the summer the steam engine was mostly able to keep the water below land level and so he had to work for the drainage commissioners of the district.

At this time, barges being the chief means of transport for heavy material about the fens, boat building and boat repairing was quite a good trade and the men that did the work were called boatwrights. There was a man living at Isleham Sluice who looked after the sluice and did the boatwright work too. To him my father was sent with some of the barges that belonged to the drainage district where he worked to help repair the barges. This gave him the chance to learn to repair boats and barges.

How long he stayed at this mill I don't quite know but after a few years he took charge and went to live in another mill. Seventeen or eighteen years after they married they were still living in a windmill with seven children, of whom I believe six were born in a mill. I wonder what people would think today about children being born in a windmill. Outside, the sails, perhaps sixty feet long, would be swinging round in the wind, the whole structure of the place shaking and creaking, the paddle wheel splashing and spluttering on the side of the house. Amid these conditions I believe four of my sisters and two brothers were born.

Changes were continually taking place in the fen. With the help of the steam engine the land was better drained and I think about this time the drainage commissioners realised the poor old windmill had had its day – or perhaps it would be kinder to the mills to say they had

had their swing. More people were coming into the fens to live and work; the land was farmed better. As more people came and the land was better drained the wildfowl, fish and otter began to leave. One by one the windmills were left derelict; some were pulled down and others were left to fall down. Today I don't think there is one windmill left in this district. There is part of the structure of one of the windmills that my father lived in still standing. After he left the sails were taken off and the structure made into a more suitable dwelling place. It is now called the "Pepper Pot".

In the year 1891 my father applied for a situation as drainage superintendent of the Mildenhall Fen. He got the job and they even built him a new house for him to live in. Here another sister and I were born and here we lived until I was seventeen years old. During this period my father taught me many things. In this position he had to look at the drainage of the fens on a much larger scale. He held this post for twenty two years. Then he took on the job of sluice keeper at Isleham Sluice and died there at the age of sixty nine in the year 1924.

A few days before he died, when he knew there was no hope of getting well again, he said to my eldest brother "Well, Jack I have had a good innings and a happy life". So you see it was possible to enjoy life even in those days.

There are to my knowledge living today more than one hundred direct descendants from Old Joe Wells and it may be there are two or three times that number – that I don't know. Anyway we are here in the year 1957 and, to the best of my knowledge, that is how we came to be here.

Chapter 2.

THE FENS DRAINED.

Many and varied were the difficult problems the early drainage engineers had to face. Apart from the financial and drainage problems there was the difficult problem of finding labourers in this sparsely populated district, a task made worse by the hostile attitude of the local inhabitants. I sympathise very deeply with those fen people. For them I should think it was almost like taking their life away to drain the fens. I do wonder now if it was worth spending so much work and money on a small part of England that could have been left in its natural state. What a lovely place it would have been for man to spend his holidays in and what a lovely place for birds and beasts to revel in and it would have cost the country nothing whereas today, after what has already been spent on it, it is costing millions of pounds. This is a very important statement because members of my family for six generations, myself included, have obtained a living by drainage work.

I suppose modernisation and progress have their good points as well as bad. We should give credit where credit is due and I firmly believe those early drainage engineers believed they were doing a good job and must have worked hard. It is rather difficult to explain how far the drainage of the fens had advanced when Old Joe Wells came into the fen. Although work had been going on for hundreds of years it does not appear that they had made much progress. The sea barrier at Denver that was called Denver Sluice was built about the year 1652 – 1653. This sluice or barrier blew up or burst in 1713 and was not rebuilt until 1749. This would be about fifty or sixty years before Joe made his appearance.

It will be understood that although Denver Sluice prevented the tides from flowing into the fens it did not stop the rain from falling in the fens or on the surrounding hills. The water from the hills had to pass through the fens. I should imagine there was sufficient water even in summer time to force a small winding channel through the soft peaty soil to the outlet at Denver. In winter, when the heavy rains and snow came, these channels would overflow and flood the whole area. Banks had to be made on each side of the channels perhaps not very high at first but high enough to prevent the water in the fen from running into the channels which we now call rivers.

This is where the windmills came in and, I would imagine, my great grandfather too. Windmills were erected along the river banks to lift the water from the fen into the rivers. Drains had to be cut to convey the water across the fens to the mills. Ditches had to be cut for the water to pass into the drains. These ditches were cut, when it was convenient according to the level of the land, so as to form square or oblong patches of the fens which we call fields – or, to use fen language, grounds. Some of the ditches were very crooked. I should think they were natural water courses cleaned out and made into ditches – a ditch by the fen men was called a dyke. The soil thrown out by cutting the ditches and drains formed a bank around the fields. These banks had to be spread by hand. This job was known as spreading the dyke bank but a man could only throw the earth about twenty or thirty feet. In a few years the outside of the fields became higher than the centre so they had to dig what were called sock grips to drain the water from the inner part of the field to the ditches. Most of this work had to be done by hand and a large number of men had to be employed who could use a spade or shovel.

They were called toolmen. I believe some of them considered themselves just a little superior to the ordinary farm worker because they worked less hours and received more pay per week but they had to find their own tools. With all this work to do, and more land being cultivated, houses and farms were built. The fens were getting more thickly populated. There was more money and public houses were built along the river bank. This was convenient for the bargemen who travelled along the rivers and also helped to empty their pockets. The wind swung the sails of the mills round; the paddle wheels splashed the water into the river; the men worked in the drains and the women did their housework or worked on the land. The fen was getting quite a busy place but, alas, the very life blood was being sucked away. As the water was drained out of this peaty soil it became more solid and settled down to a lower level.

This brought new problems for the drainage engineers to face because, not only did the level of the fens get lower but, with all the mills pumping water into the rivers, the level of water in the rivers got higher. In the wet periods the extra water coming down from the hills made it necessary to raise and strengthen the banks. This made more work for the men and barges and more money for the labourers and innkeepers. More stress and strain was put on the poor old windmills because they had to lift the water higher. I think it ought to be said here that the engineers solved the problem for themselves and the mills. When it was found too much for one mill to lift the water into the river another mill was erected a short distance away. The new mill would lift the water from the fen into what was called the mill raft; the old mill lifting the water from the mill raft into the river, thereby sharing the work between them. These mills were called the double lift mills. It was into one of these double lift mills that my father went to live when he was married.

The fens being continually drained, they settled lower and lower. It was getting too much for the mills to lift the water into the river. Something had to be done about it so the steam engine was introduced to the fens and steam driven pumping stations were built to take the place of the mills. They were a big improvement; great strides were being made in the drainage of the fens. Here, again, history repeated itself. The more the fens were drained, the more they settled and the more water there was pumped into the river. The banks had to be made higher and stronger. It soon became apparent that after a period of very wet weather the banks would be in great danger of overflowing or even bursting and flooding large areas of the fens. So it was necessary in flood time for men to keep a strict watch on the banks for any sign of overflowing or a breach in the banks.

In was not an uncommon sight when I was a lad to see lights moving slowly along the banks after dark; candle or oil lanterns were mostly used for this purpose. If you had met one of these lights on the bank you would have seen that it was carried by a man. He would also be carrying a shovel for his work was to stop the water running over the bank and to watch out for any sign of a breach in the bank. Any unusual occurrence he would report to the local drainage engineer. If he thought it necessary he would warn the inhabitants of that area to get their stock and themselves on to higher land. But first he had to make sure what the trouble was and, if possible, put it right. This watching the bank would go on until the water returned to what was considered a safe level. Very often by that time one of the banks would have burst and relieved the pressure on the rest of the banks till the flood was over.

The coming of the engine was the death of the windmills although a few of them carried on for a time along the river bank. A few small mills were built in the lower part of the fen to pump the water out of the ditches into the drains but they did not last long. About this time quite a number of men were digging up the peaty soil, drying it and selling it for fuel. This helped to lower the level of the fen.

In 1914 the Great War came. More of the fen land was ploughed up. When left fallow in summer the surface of this peaty soil would actually turn into dust and, if the wind was strong, the dust would be blown high into the air. If you looked at these dust storms from a mile or so distant they looked very much like thunderstorms. All this helped in the shrinkage of the fen soil. Soon after the war there was a revolution in fen drainage and great changes took place. Powerful diesel engines with centrifugal pumps were brought into the fen and they soon put the steam engine out of action. Not only were they able to pump more water and lift it higher but they were able to do it in a much shorter time. In the rivers could be seen the powerful dredgers lifting mud from the bottom of the river, their jibs swinging round and putting it on top of the banks, so deepening the rivers and making the banks higher. In the fens could be seen small dragline dredgers deepening the drains and ditches.

In a few years machines were doing most of the work that before had been done by hand, and doing it much more quickly. The fens were drained to such a low level that the paddle wheel of the old steam engine was left high and dry. About this time iron barges could be seen being drawn along the rivers by small motor tugs, taking the place of the horse-drawn wooden barges, loaded with clay from rossel pits to make the banks stronger – this clay was called gault by the fen men. The fens were being drained so much that there was little peat suitable for fuel; coal had become more plentiful so the turf business went out with the steam engine. Manual work became slack and, in this part of the fens, the inhabitants began to drift away. There was less traffic along the rivers. The public houses began to go out of action so that in one stretch of the river of two miles there is now only one where there had been four – so perhaps the fen is being drained of beer as well as of water. Not only public houses went out of action but also two schools and two small chapels.

With all this machinery and powerful pumping stations the fens are being drained to such an extent that the surface of the fenland is now below the water level of the river. I suppose in flood time the fen is about ten or twelve feet below the water in the river but THE FENS ARE DRAINED. Some people say they are drained too much for the good of the land but this is a matter of opinion. My opinion is that, if any thing is doing at all, it is worth doing well and, in the year 1957, I believe the fens are drained well – but are not safe by any means. I am afraid that if I lived in the fens today I would not sleep very soundly in flood time. Nor do I believe the fens will ever be safe while the water from hills has to pass through them. I believe the drainage engineers have proposed cutting a new river (if it is not already started*) to catch and convey the water from the hills around the edge of the fens to the sea without passing through the fens. When this is done I think that it will be a big step towards making the fens safe from floods. The fens are cultivated; good crops are harvested and roads have been made in all directions. Dry land is here where once fish, birds, reptiles and men lived and enjoyed themselves.

(*The cut-off channel from Barton Mills to Denver Sluice, part of the Great Ouse flood protection scheme, was completed in September 1964.)

Chapter 3

NAVIGATION.

Navigation and drainage have always been very closely connected in the fens; water traffic was the chief, if not the only, means of transporting heavy goods about the fens. When the fens were being drained it was found necessary to build sluices and staunches along the upper reaches of the river to hold the water up high enough to float the barges. This also served to irrigate the fens in summer time if necessary. The banks along the river, which were made to keep the water out of the fen, made excellent towing paths so the horse-drawn barges or gangs took the place of the sailing boats.

The word gang was used when three or four or more barges or boats were fixed together one behind the other in such a manner that, although they were drawn by a horse walking on the bank, they could be steered along the channel of the river. The wooden barges at that time were called lighters and they would be able to carry anything from eight to thirty tons. Very often these gangs would consist of four lighters, a horse boat capable of carrying about four tons and a dinghy, called by the watermen a cox boat. The horse boat was used for ferrying the horse across the river where necessary. The cox boat was used when the water was too shallow for the lighters to get close to the bank. It would be propelled by a man standing up in the stern of the boat using a scull, a rather ticklish job which had to be practised before it could be done properly.

There was usually a cabin in one of the lighters, very often in the stem or centre of the second lighter. If in the stem it would be almost triangular in shape with sides about eight feet, a small fireplace inside and a thick glass skylight at the top. If the cabin was in the centre of the lighter it would be about eight or nine feet square with a small wooden window on either side and about five and half feet high. Sometimes the men would live on these gangs for weeks at a time but the cabins had to be registered before they were allowed to live in them. Sometimes the gangs would travel thirty or forty miles with a load, unload, take another load travel somewhere else and unload and away again. Most of the produce of the fens was carried by the gangs. Corn would be carried to the water-driven grinding mills on the upper reaches of the rivers. There was quite a lot of clunch or chalk and gravel carried from the hills into the fens for making roads and coal had to be carried for the steam engines. It is well to note here that the drainage engineers had to work with the navigation authorities. Water had to be kept at a certain level at the sluices and staunches for at some of the sluices there would be a drop of four or five feet.

The horses pulling the gangs were called gang horses. There was so much traffic by these gang horses along the banks that the drainage people had to charge them tolls for the damage they did to the banks. The south level district was divided into several small local drainage areas, each of them charging a toll, so there were quite a number of tolls.

I suppose it would be difficult for most people today to understand the meaning of the equipment of these gangs or the language of the old watermen. Forty years ago, as sluice keeper, it was not unusual for me to hear something like this when the gang horse reached the pen. The master of the gang would shout, and he had to shout because he would be about sixty or seventy yards away, "Unhook. Hook your trace up. Take his bits out. Loose his rein. Let yer hoss have a feed. Get ready to close the door". These orders would be for the horse driver. The master of the gang would be standing in the centre of the pole lighter against the steering pole, guiding the gang into the pen. He would then say to the second in command "Put the fenders out. Pull the rope in". As soon as the stem of the forelighter was in the pen he would shout "Make the pole fast. Come forward and roll against the wall of the pen to stop the lighter from banging against the wall." Then he would shout to the second man "Take your cordbys off.

Loose the seising fests. Shove the jarm pole back. Uncouple 'em. Get on the third lighter. Make that short rope fast to the kimblent. Jump out and take a turn round that post. Don't let her bang, she may be yours one day".

All this time the master would be busy steadying the forelighter in the pen and making a rope fast to the kimblent of the forelighter, getting out and taking a one turn round the post. By taking one turn of the rope round a post it was possible to steady the boats up without banging them. When two of the lighters were in the pen the lower doors would be closed, the pen filled up, the top doors opened and the lighters pulled out. Then the top doors were closed, the pen emptied and the lower doors opened. The whole operation was repeated until all the gang was through the sluice.

When this was done the master of the gang would usually slip a shilling or two into the hand of the sluicekeeper and say quietly "Keep us a good water". The sluicekeeper would reply, all in good faith, "I'll do the best I can for you", knowing all the time he was not allowed to hold the water above a certain level. However there were lots of ways he could help them so I think both parties were happy about it. There was not always a lot of noise with a well-equipped gang and an efficient crew. To a casual observer these lighters would seem to glide into the pen almost automatically, each man doing his job properly and at the right time, working together almost like a machine. The master of the gang, though not saying anything, would be watching every movement. Anyone looking on would have to watch very closely to see a good tip pass from the gang master to the sluicekeeper. It was very nice to see how some of these men could handle barges but it was awful to see how some of the barges were banged about by men who didn't know how to manage them.

I feel I ought to say a word here about the poor old gang horses.. Some of them, apart from their work, had to sleep in a different stable almost every night and the work was hard. They could only travel about two miles an hour so they had to walk very slowly, pulling on one shoulder nearly all the time. This caused sore shoulders in lots of cases. They were very often driven by a strong lad about fifteen or sixteen years old. In some cases they were lads with no homes, taken out of the workhouse for that purpose. These drivers had to keep a strict watch on the horse to see that it did not turn off the towing path or bank and they had to walk behind the horse so that they could keep the line clear of stakes or bushes. If the line got foul the barges would be pulled into the bank and stop the gang, very often causing a long delay and a lot of shouting and swearing too.

At stages along the banks there were fences to separate bunches of cattle belonging to different people. The gang horse had to learn to jump these fences. It was not too bad for them when they were used to it but I am afraid they were treated rather rough in the learning stage. When they came to a fence the horse had to stop for a minute or two to allow sufficient slack line for it to jump the fence. It also had to learn to jump into the horseboat to be ferried across the river when necessary. These horses, through having to travel so slowly when pulling the gang, would soon develop a habit of going forward two or three steps and then steadying up for a second or two till the rope became slack, then forward another step or two. This particular habit was known as the "Bury Walk". I imagine it was called that because it was more noticeable along the River Lark that runs down from Bury St. Edmunds. My father thought it was because this river had a lot of turns and the current was usually rather strong.

Apart from these gangs of large lighters there were gangs of smaller boats carrying about eight tons each. These eight ton boats were usually used by the drainage commissioners to carry gault from the rossel pits to make up the banks or to carry chalk from the higher bank for the same purpose. In a gang of eight ton boats the cabin would generally be in the stern of the second boat. It would be about six feet square with a small stove – quite cosy little cabins they were too. I well remember my first day at school. My brother was working on one of these gangs and they were passing our house and going nearly as far as the school so I was put aboard and made nice and comfortable in the cabin. We had to travel about two and half miles to school so it was about an hour's ride. I enjoyed the ride much better than the rest of the day at school.

I have heard my father say that in his young time they used gangs of smaller boats carrying about four tons each. These smaller boats were used sometimes in the fen drains for carrying turf and other materials about the fens. When a drain was cut across a drove – all roadways in the fen were green droves in those days – a wooden bridge was put across the drain high and wide enough for these four ton boats to pass under. My father had good reason to remember one of these bridges. I have heard him tell a tale about something that happened to him when he and others were skating along the drains. I believe they were coming home from a skating match. When they came to one of these bridges they had to stoop to go under the bridge but father did not stoop low enough. He bumped his head against the bridge and, as he was travelling at speed, he sat down very quickly. Unfortunately it cracked his head. When he told this tale he would bend down and show his bald head so you could see the scar forty years later.

Most of the gangs carried a dag for spearing pike or other fish and a glaive for catching eels. These fish were cooked in the little cabin and eaten there.

There were a few steam-driven tugs travelling about the river but not many. They did not seem to become popular in this district, perhaps because there was not enough space in the rivers for them to manoeuvre properly. They were mostly long narrow tugs requiring a good depth of water. It may seem impossible today but I have heard my father say that one of the steam tugs once went up the River Lark as far as Bury St. Edmunds. It was called "The Cutter" and I think it was a special trip more for publification than anything else. Most of the bargemen seemed to prefer the old gang horse for haulage. Of course there were always the pleasure sailing yachts cluttering up the rivers with their tall masts and big sails, getting in the way of the useful river traffic.

These things happened before the 1914 – 1918 War. After the war, as in other forms of transport, there was a great change in the navigation. Iron barges took the place of the wooden lighters and boats. Small motor tugs were used in place of the gang horses. There was no skill in navigating these iron barges. If they knocked against each other, or against the concrete wall of the sluices, they would just shudder and bounce away and that is about all the harm it did. When the wooden barges bumped it was a different matter. The old watermen soon found it was impossible to carry on under these conditions. In my opinion the real art of navigation on the fen rivers has passed away. A few of the iron gangs are still in use, chiefly for carrying clay to repair the bank and for carrying sugar beet to the factory at Ely. Very often they are loaded and unloaded by crane or by grab dredger so there is little hand labour involved. Maybe it is good that men do not have to work as hard as they did but I am convinced there is not so much interest in the work or half as much pleasure got out of it as there was in the old days.

There are still a few pleasure boats about the rivers in summer, mostly motor boats about twenty to thirty feet long with cabins. Some are fitted out very nicely and are well handled but it is horrifying to watch how some of these boats are handled by men who appear to know nothing about the job at all.

Miss Annie Wells on the bank of the River Lark below Alder Farm in March 1937. The bank was in danger of giving way with the high water level.

The author and his family skating at the Isleham Ferry House in February 1936. Under the ice was a field of winter wheat which gave an excellent yield when harvested.

The River Lark at Wamil. 1908.

A gang of Mildenhall Fen Drainage Board lighters in 1913 – on the River Lark between Cross Bank and the Cock Inn.

So it seems that the navigation of the fen rivers has passed away like almost all the old trades of the fen and will soon be completely forgotten. Like the old windmills they seemed to rise out of the swamp and mud to become very useful and the men became very skilled in these trades but, as the water was drained out of the land and it became more solid, these trades and crafts just faded out and are remembered no more. Still the result of their labour and usefulness can be seen today for they all had their day and played their parts in the drainage of the fens. Instead of water, swamp and mud we see today wonderful crops of corn, sugarbeet, potatoes, celery and flowers produced by this very fertile soil.

Chapter 4.

TOOLMEN OR TRADESMEN OF THE FEN.

It would be almost impossible to look back on the history of the drainage of the fens without the toolmen looming up in big characters before you. They were strong, hardy and skilled men although quite often they were unable to read or write. I said in one of the earlier chapters that I believe some of these toolmen considered themselves superior to the ordinary farmworker. Maybe they had reason to be – in my opinion they were far more skilled than some of the so called engineers of today. They not only had to be masters of several trades and know how to use quite a number of tools but in lots of cases they made some of their own tools. In fact a good toolman was expected by his employer to be able to turn his hand to almost any kind of work in the fens. He was expected to be able to work by himself or with a gang of men. A gang of men in the fen language means a number of men working together as one unit with one leading man called a ganger or foreman. The ganger usually did the talking for the men to the employer and also for the employer to the men and agreed about the price for the work that was to be done – not a very thankful office sometimes. Although he was in charge and told the other men what to do he had not the authority to discharge them from their work and in lots of cases he received no extra pay.

A toolman's outfit would generally consist of something like this:–

> A pair of leather boots costing about
> as much as he could earn in 36 days;
> A small bundle of hay;
> A thin stick about 15 inches long for
> stuffing the hay in his boots;
> A small tin of grease for the boots &
> A file wrapped in a small sack.

When he stopped work at night, they were all put in a bag and buried, the whole gang putting their bags in one common grave. This stopped the boots from freezing during the night. If he was working in a drain or ditch by himself, or if he was likely to take a ganger's place, he would need a moor spade, chrome, a four-tined fork, shovel, water scoop and scythe. These would cost him about as much as he could earn in 14 days. If he was claying he would need a flytool. One day's work might be turf digging and for this he would need a becket, costing another day's work. If he was roading ditches he would need a roading scythe, stick and rake – another three day's work – and perhaps a two-tined fork and hatchet – three more days' work. There would probably be other tools he would need but this lot would cost him in all about as much as he could earn in ten weeks, so you could almost call him a capitalist.

I well remember when I was a lad sitting around the fire in the kitchen of the then almost new tall house, with my mother and sisters and sometimes my brother, listening to the stories my father would tell about his early days. Perhaps we would be clipping a piece of willow to make chain pins for eel hives, or maybe just talking, when something would remind my father of certain happenings when he was young. It might be the mention of someone's name or perhaps one of us would say "I heard today that old Mr. So-and-So is dead." I think my father was a good talker. He would perhaps start off something like this: "Well, he was a nice chap when you got to know him. I remember working with him in a drain somewhere." Then he would to on to describe where the drain was or tell us something about the man or what he did.

It would seem that they had a bit of fun in the gangs sometimes. When a young man joined a gang for the first time it seemed to have been the rule that he had to be shod. That is to say he had to pay for a certain amount of beer before he was considered a proper toolman. If he would not pay willingly he was held by two or three men whilst another would knock a nail through the sole of his shoe until he called "Beer" – and of course that meant he was willing to pay. Then one of the men would go off to the nearest pub for a fetching of beer, which of course did not last long. So they had to think of some other way of getting more. In some gangs I think it was a rule that, if a man joined a gang after the first day, he was expected to pay for a certain amount of beer – a kind of entrance fee to the gang. Sometimes it was a rule that if a man appeared for work on a Monday without a clean dummy he was fined a halfpenny of a penny. A dummy, by the way, was a kind of shirt which they wore as an overall to stop their other clothes from getting splashed with mud.

The gang made their own rules so, if they could not get enough money one way, they would make another rule. I believe it was a rule in some gangs to fine a man for every swear word he said on the job and also for breaking wind. The pennies and halfpennies in a large gang soon made up for a fetching of beer because, if a man made a single slip, you may be sure he was not able to get out of it without paying. When working in the drains there was always the money that the fish sales made. It was a general rule in all gangs that any fish caught on the work should be kept till leaving-off time, usually in a hole dug in the ground and covered over, and then sold by auction. One of the gang would act as auctioneer and another as clerk; all accounts had to be settled on pay day and the money was usually spent on beer.

By the time I was old enough to work in a gang it was paid out in equal shares.

It was acting as a clerk to one of these gangs that my father did his first job of book-keeping.

I well remember my first day working in a drain with a gang of men. I went with my brother. We had to cycle about four miles and when we arrived at the drain some of the old hands were booting up – that is putting on their long thigh boots and stuffing them up with hay. This usually took about a quarter of an hour. There was quite a lot of bantering and pulling my leg but the shoeing business had just about died out by that time so I did not have to pay for beer.

When we got in the drain I had to work in the front because a new hand usually splashes a lot of mud and water about before he gets used to the work and they did not want to get smothered. I had been given to understand beforehand that I was expected to do my share of the work. I was quite young, about sixteen I think, so I worked as hard as I could all day. I expect I made a poor go of it but I at least worked hard and was very glad when it was time to stop work and go home to a nice hot meal.

My weariness was nothing compared to how I felt next morning. I was stiff and sore all over. I just felt that I wanted to lie still and not move a finger; the thought of getting out of bed was terrible. I had slept with my brother. He jumped out of bed and seemed quite fresh. I did not want him or the other men to know how I felt although I think he had some idea that I had worked a little too hard the day before. I got up and had my breakfast. I did not want to go to work but I dared not give up and say I could not do it so I just had to go. When we got to work I felt so bad and my hands were sore and blistered. I had a subconscious feeling that the men were all watching me to see how I would react. I think that prompted me to work again so I continued working as hard as I could. After a few days the stiffness began to go; the blisters broke and were much easier. Before very long I realised I was able to scoop the water without splashing and to throw the soft mud out of the drain in one lump with spattering it all over the place. I could move about in the mud more easily and on the whole I was able to work harder and more comfortably. Ditching and draining work never seemed so hard to me after that.

In a gang of ten or twenty of these toolmen there were many different characters. Perhaps some very rough men, some devoted Christians and some so keen about money as to be almost miserly. Yet they all seemed to be able to work together comfortably to the advantage of the gang and to have a reasonably good time. There was something about the toolmen that I cannot explain or even understand. There was so much individuality about them for they all had their own characters which showed up plainly but the other members of the gang seemed to recognise these different natures and to accept them.

If one of the men went on a spree and got drunk, and did not turn up for several days, no one seemed to take much notice of it. It was taken to be the general run of things. If one of them was preaching at the chapel on Sunday it just went as a matter of course; no-one seemed to pay much attention to it. If one of them came to work on Monday with a black eye through fighting on Saturday night there might be a few critical glances in his direction but, aside from that, it just seemed a part of the way of life and things went on as usual. It might even have been a fight between two men doing the same kind of work. Was it because they thought the cause of the fight wasn't worth showing enmity or was it because they had had their fight and knocked the enmity out of each other? I believe it was something that is difficult to explain – a happy go lucky superior individuality; an independent self reliance mingled with a spirit of co-operation, that made them able to fight each other and yet work together.

I remember when I was quite young my brother had a fight with a man on the Saturday night. Somehow their caps got mixed up and my brother came home with the wrong cap. On the Monday my sister and I had to go to the man's home and get them changed. I don't think we liked it very much but, there it was, it had to be done.

I think it was the individual independence of these men that made them stand out so clearly in my mind.

Each man was a separate unit. So long as he did his work he did not fear his workmates or his employer. If anything went wrong there was no union to which to appeal. It was between the man and his employer whether he stood or fell. Usually he stood for, if the employer complained about his work, he would very often face up to him and say "If you are not satisfied you can jolly well do it yourself" – only he would use more determined and aggressive adjectives. Then he would calmly collect his tools, pack them up and leave. It did not worry him and he would probably go the nearest pub and have a drink, perhaps get drunk. Unlike the farm labourer who, if he lost his job, lost his house too and had to find a new one, the toolman only had to find another job; so you see he was in a slightly superior position to the farmworker.

At that time, when nearly all the drainage work was done by hand, it was not much trouble for a man to get employment if he was willing to work. If he had been afraid of work he would not have been a toolman. He was not a part of anything; when he spoke of his employer he did not say "my master" or "our farm" as though he belonged to it. He was a separate unit although he co-operated with the gang when he worked with it. He was not subservient to it. There was always this individualism about him although he would perhaps soon be back with his old employer again.

Another thing which promoted independence was that a good number of these old toolmen, at least in this district, had some form of sideline to bring in a small income apart from their work. Some had been in the army and were receiving a small amount of reserve pay; some would mend shoes in their spare time; some would make scoops or scythe sticks; some had a piece of land. When I was at school there was a field in Isleham Fen let in one acre plots for the turf to be dug out in five years. These plots were mostly hired by toolmen who dug their own turfs in their own time, dried them and sold them in the villages. If they were busy their wives would go round the village with a load of turf, hawking it. Some of them lived in public houses, their wives looking after the pubs whilst they were at work. Looking back at some of the characters I knew I cannot help noting that there was a good percentage of bachelors amongst them so they had only themselves to keep.

As a last resort there was always the poaching business. If these strong hardy men could not earn a living by day they could make sure of an existence by going out poaching at night – and who could blame them? Hunger, I am told, is a sharp pain made more severe when they could see their children suffering for lack of food. Often it meant poaching or taking something that belonged to somebody else. Perhaps it was wrong to poach but I think they chose the lesser evil in this case. What was wrong with taking a net out and catching some of the wild birds that were there in abundance, some of which were in fact a nuisance to the farmers and landlords? If a partridge or pheasant got mixed up in the bag, well, good luck to the poachers. What they got by poaching was hard-earned money and I think most of the men would rather have been at work if they could.

While most of the drainage work in the fens was done by hand I don't think the toolmen suffered much through unemployment while the weather was reasonably good. Always at the back of their minds there was the dread of the bugbear of the fens – frost and snow. The frost turned the fens into a solid block, land and water too; the snow came and covered it with a mantle of white, like wrapping up a dead thing in shroud. As one looked around there was the weird feeling that the level whiteness, stretching as far as the eye could see in almost all directions, was unending. Gazing into this utter emptiness, with cold chills creeping down your back and your feet and hands beginning to turn numb with cold, a deadly nothingness seemed to take hold of you as though you were a part of this emptiness and your spirit was in the elements. You turned and faced the west and there you saw just above the skyline the silhouette of that great and wonderful monument of the fens, Ely Cathedral. This sight moved you back to earth; your spirit rejoined your body and you became real again. Yet you were filled with awe and admiration for that great monument has been there for hundreds of years and has passed through many storms frosts and snows and is still there; and you think "Soon the frost and snow will be gone and we shall have normal conditions again". But, while it lasted, nearly all the work in the fen was dead.

Some of the people kept warm by skating about on the flat surface of the water; some were interested in skating matches; some of the men preferred the cosy tap room of the pub. All knew that, after the frost and snow, the floods would come, making more work for everybody, perhaps night work as well as day – watching banks, etc.

In the spring there was the seasonal farmwork such as hoeing corn and forking twitch. Most of the extra farmwork was done by the toolmen. Looking at it from a general point of view, I suppose the toolman was in a fairly good position in his day.

Another point about them was that they nearly all liked their beer. Most of them could find enough money to get drunk on Saturday nights. I heard a story about one old chap who told a tale about a special job he was on somewhere where the employer supplied plenty of beer. He said there was so much he drank all he could until he just couldn't drink anymore. He said "My will was good enough but I couldn't drink any more". I think it seemed a tragedy to him that the beer was there and he could not drink it.

These toolmen all lived and worked before the 1914–18 War. After the war machinery came in and did a lot of the work that had been done by hand. The days of the toolmen were past. A lot of them were crippled or maimed for life. Some tried to carry on with croaky chests but modern machinery soon took their place, They, like the windmills, were soon forgotten and so passed out a noble hardworking set of men. There are still a few of the old toolmen living today but not many. Most of them that are living are past the retiring age and unable to get about much.

Do they rejoice in the result of their labours? Far from it. If you hear them talk it seems the result of their work does not count at all but they seem to get a certain amount of pleasure out of the memory of what they did. Instead of saying "Look at those lovely crops; I remember when that old land was nearly always flooded, would grow anything only grass" they would often say something like this: "Do you remember working in the old engine drain when old what's-his-name broke his scoop trying to get that big eel?; you ought to have heard him in the pub that night; that was when old Mrs. So-and-So kept it; what a difference now; we had some good do's then; we used to work then; yes, and fight; they don't know what work is today; all they think about is having off-time. Ah, I was wondering the other day how long it is ago since old what's-his-name fell overboard and they wouldn't stop the hoss to get him aboard. Yes, he had a rare ducking that day. Let's see; that was afore his wife died and she has been dead forty year this summer. He was lucky he worn't drowned that day."

They seemed to lose themselves in the past and forget the present. We work hard for something when we are young; when we are old we forget that for which we have worked.

NOTES